The Sustainable Wedding

Plan Your Big Day with the Earth in Mind

Table of Contents

Chapter 1. Introduction

Welcome to our Special Report: The Sustainable Wedding: Plan Your Big Day with the Earth in Mind. This guide features a collection of tips, expert insights, and heartwarming stories that'll help you to celebrate the love of your life while also honoring the love you have for our planet. More than a simple wedding planning guide, this Special Report is your compendium to prepare an unforgettable, visually stunning event that's also socially conscious and environmentally friendly. Say 'I do' to a beautiful, memorable, and sustainable wedding, all while setting a standard for eco-friendly celebrations that could inspire others. Green is the new white for weddings, embark on this journey of love and sustainability with us today!

Chapter 2. Defining a Sustainable Wedding: Why it Matters

The concept of a sustainable wedding revolves around orchestrating an entire event, from the announcement to the farewell brunch, in a conscious manner that minimises harm to the environment. It's about fostering love, not just between two individuals but also for Mother Earth, as we reconsider our options and adopt alternatives that can significantly lessen our ecological footprint.

2.1. What is a sustainable wedding?

A sustainable wedding, also known as a green wedding or eco-wedding, is a wedding planned with eco-friendly considerations at the forefront. It involves making choices that minimize the environmental impact of the event, from the invitations you send to the food you serve, the transportation you use, and the items you purchase.

The implications of a sustainable wedding are far-reaching. By choosing to plan a sustainable wedding, you're choosing to reduce waste, to support local businesses and fair trade, to prioritize energy-efficient logistics, and in most instances, to endorse cruelty-free, organic, and non-toxic products.

2.2. Why sustainable weddings matter

Sustainable weddings may reduce harm to the environment, but they also contribute positively in different ways.

2.2.1. Impact on Environment

The average wedding produces 400 lbs. of waste and 63 tons of CO2. With over 2.4 million weddings every year in the U.S. alone, an immense amount of waste accumulates, contributing significantly to environmental degradation. The choice of a sustainable wedding mitigates this harm, reducing the event's carbon footprint and waste produced.

2.2.2. Support for Local Economies

Sustainable weddings often involve sourcing locally produced items, which effectively boosts local economies. From locally grown flowers and food to handmade decors, sustainable weddings encourage brides and grooms to shop small, creating an economic ripple effect in their communities.

2.2.3. Setting a Positive Example

Opting for a sustainable wedding sets an influential example for wedding guests and onlookers. It can inspire others to follow suit, to see weddings (and gatherings in general) in a different light, appreciating the romance and beauty in being eco-friendly.

2.3. Major components of a sustainable wedding

A sustainable wedding integrates eco-friendly options into every aspect of the event. Here are the major components to consider:

2.3.1. Eco-friendly Invitations

The first point of contact between the couple and the guests are the invitations. Opt for digital invites or select stationery made from recycled materials or other eco-friendly options.

2.3.2. Sustainable Venue

Choosing a venue that supports sustainability or a natural setting that requires minimal decoration can save resources. Look for venues with sustainable practices in place or open spaces like gardens or vineyards which have a natural ambiance.

2.3.3. Local and Seasonal Food

Food and beverages at a sustainable wedding should ideally come from local, organic sources. Serving seasonal cuisine not only reduces carbon emissions due to transportation but also offers the freshest and tastiest options.

2.3.4. Earth-friendly Attire

Bridal wear can reflect your commitment to sustainability as well. Consider wedding dresses and suits made of sustainable fabrics or explore the option of vintage or second-hand clothing.

2.3.5. Ethical Rings

Choose rings made from ethically sourced or recycled materials. Many jewelers offer beautiful options made out of fair trade gold or reused precious metals.

2.3.6. Green Decor

Decor at a sustainable wedding should be minimized and as natural as possible. Use locally grown flowers, potted plants, and other reusable, bio-degradable materials.

2.3.7. Low-impact Transportation

Consider transportation options that reduce carbon emissions: carpooling, shuttle buses for guests, or even bicycles if distances are short.

2.4. Conclusion

In the grand scheme of a lifetime commitment, a single day of celebration might seem miniscule. But choices we make for this one day can echo into the future, influencing not just our lives but also our world at large. A sustainable wedding isn't just a trend; it's a lasting statement about your perspective, a testament to the fact that love for your partner and love for the Earth aren't mutually exclusive.

As we move towards the impending environmental crisis, every choice and commitment matter. Let your wedding be the start of a conscious future, a testament to sustainable yet stylish living. Remember, defining a sustainable wedding isn't complicated, it only requires a willing mind, loving heart, and a respect for the Earth we share.

Stay tuned as we journey together towards creating your dream, green wedding. We'll explore each aspect in detail, providing you with practical tips, foolproof advice, industry insights and heartwarming stories to inspire your eco-conscious big day.

Chapter 3. The Green Engagement: Eco-friendly Rings and Proposals

An engagement is often marked by an exchange of rings, symbolizing a promise of future matrimony and lifelong commitment. Over time, engagement rings have evolved from simple bands exchanged by ancient Egyptians to dazzling diamond-studded pieces that scream expensive taste and classic style. However, as you embark on your sustainable wedding journey, it's important to consider the environmental impact and ethical concerns related to diamond mining and other methods of traditional jewelry manufacture.

3.1. Ethical Diamond Mining and Eco-friendly Alternatives

When it comes to choosing your diamond, it's important to select one that has been mined responsibly. This means ensuring the stone was sourced from a location that upholds proper worker rights, fair wages, and doesn't contribute significantly to environmental degradation. Look for retailers who abide by the Kimberley Process standards, an international resolution aimed at preventing the flow of conflict diamonds.

Lab-grown diamonds are another excellent, eco-friendly alternative. Scientifically indistinguishable from mined diamonds, these stones are created in a controlled lab environment, thus they require far less energy and natural resources to produce. Not only do synthetic diamonds decrease demand for diamond mining, but they are also typically less expensive.

Moissanite, a naturally occurring mineral, is another sustainable choice. Moissanite is rare in nature, but can be lab-grown, emitting less carbon and requiring fewer resources than diamond mining. Because of its sparkly attributes, it's often compared to diamonds and can be a more affordable and equally beautiful alternative.

3.2. Choosing Eco-friendly Metals

For the band of your engagement ring, sustainable options exist too. Common materials like gold and silver are often mined in environmentally destructive ways. To counter this, look for Fairmined certified gold, which guarantees the gold was mined under rigorous environmental and social conditions.

Recycled metals are another viable alternative. These metals are reclaimed from various sources - including existing jewelry items, industrial-use metals, and electronics - and reworked into new pieces. Using recycled metals reduces demand for new metal mining and the resulting impact on the environment.

3.3. The Eco-friendly Proposal

An eco-friendly proposal ideally integrates respect for the environment in both its planning and execution. Consider the following elements:

1. Location: Opt for an outdoor location that involves little to no travel. Local parks, a beach or your own backyard can be wonderful venues. Minimize your carbon footprint by walking, biking, or using public transportation to reach the destination.

2. Décor: Use items you already have or source from thrift stores for any decorating needs. If you're bringing flowers, make sure they're locally grown and pesticide-free, or better yet, pick wildflowers.

3. Celebrations: If you are planning a celebration afterwards,

consider making it a small, intimate gathering to reduce your ecological footprint. Choose locally sourced food and drinks, use reusable crockery and cutlery, and consider vegetarian or vegan delicacies.

3.4. Celebrating With Experience Gifts

While the engagement ring is by tradition the main event of a proposal, there is a growing trend of celebrating engagements with the gift of an experience. This might involve a wine tasting, cooking class, or a couple's spa day. An experience gift can still make the moment special and memorable, without the need for physical goods.

Being aware of the environmental impact of your decisions can keep your engagement process eco-friendly and enjoyable. This is not only beneficial for Mother Earth but can also contribute to the one-of-a-kind story of your love.

3.5. A New Normal: Setting Eco-conscious Trends

Choosing to have a green engagement can play a role in more than just preserving the environment. It also sends a message to your guests, on the importance of sustainability and intentional living. In this way, you're not just celebrating your love but also setting a trend for eco-friendly practices among your circle. This is the power of your green engagement. You're not just saying 'yes' to your partner, but also to a more sustainable future.

Planning an engagement that embodies your values of environmental responsibility is the first step to your sustainable wedding journey. It not only paves your path towards a beautiful, memorable, and sustainable wedding but also towards a better world. On this note, take a moment to cherish your commitment to one another and your commitment to our planet. May your love story inspire the hearts of many, and your green engagement set a precedent that sparks sustainable changes in the world of weddings.

It's time we consider a shift, a shift where love is not just celebrated with diamonds and grand gestures, but with mindful choices that can make a big difference. This is the essence of a 'Green Engagement.' It won't just ring in the start of your new journey with your loved one, but also the beginning of a greener tradition.

Remember, every choice matters. So, let's make our choices count. Choose love, choose sustainability, and say 'Yes' to a green engagement.

Chapter 4. Choosing the Perfect Green Venue

One of the foundational choices that you'll make when planning a sustainable wedding is the venue. This decision significantly influences your wedding's overall carbon footprint and overall sustainability. Here's how you can tread lightly with your venue choice while creating a unique and beautiful event.

4.1. Consider the Location

We begin with the fundamental question—where should your green venue be? It's not merely about the geographic location, rather, inherent characteristics that make it a sustainable option.

One aspect to consider is the distance your guests need to travel to reach your wedding destination. Is it in a city where most of the attendees live, or is it a remote location that would require long-haul flights and hotel stays? The general rule of thumb is to select a site closer to majority of your guests to reduce the carbon emissions associated with travel. Not to mention, it also adds convenience to your guests' experience.

Choose a venue that's easily accessible by public transportation, or that offers shuttle services from a central location. Encourage your guests to carpool or use electric vehicles, if available, making the transportation to your wedding as green as your intended venue.

4.2. Outdoor vs Indoor Venues

Next, let's delve into the Indoor vs. Outdoor debate. Both come with their pros and cons from a sustainability perspective.

Outdoor weddings can often require less energy for lighting and air conditioning, naturally reducing the carbon footprint. Such venues inherently carry the beauty of nature, reducing the need for additional decorations, which result in cost savings as well as conservation. However, unpredictable weather can be an issue that could lead to the use of heaters or coolers, plastic coverings for rainproofing, and other less sustainable practices.

Indoor venues, on the other hand, offer more predictability and control over the event. Classically, indoor venues haven't been as energy-efficient as we'd like them to be, but with new advancements, green buildings are no longer a rarity. Buildings equipped with energy-saving measures such as efficient heating, cooling, lighting systems, and powered by renewable energy can be a great choice for a sustainable wedding.

4.3. Certification Matters

When exploring potential venues, a valid way of determining their commitment to sustainability is by looking into their certifications. LEED-certified buildings, or those awarded certifications by local green building councils, usually guarantee standard ecological practices, which include the usage of efficient devices, materials, and practices, among other things.

Additionally, seek venues that follow other sustainable practices like waste management, water conservation, and sourcing local products and services. These aspects may not always come with a certificate but are equally important in ensuring a green event.

4.4. Nature is Your Friend

Take advantage of the natural surroundings as much as possible. Hosting an event in a botanical garden, farm, forest, or beach can add not only to the charm of the event but to your sustainable effort as well.

As a choice of venue, consider national or state parks. Such venues are deeply committed to conservation; they almost always practice the best sustainable policies and provide a sense of tranquility and purity, making them perfect for a green wedding.

4.5. Utilizing In-House Resources

Selecting a venue which provides in-house resources like furniture, sound systems, and kitchen facilities could also significantly cut down the carbon footprint of your event.

Renting these items elsewhere usually means they need to travel from the rental company to the venue contributing to more carbon emissions. Having these facilities on-site reduces transport requirements and can shave critical margins off your carbon footprint.

4.6. The All-In-One Venue

An All-In-One venue refers to a place that can host both the ceremony and the reception. These types of venues reduce transportation needs between locations and turn out to be both economically friendly and eco-friendly. Moreover, they often offer packages including catering and decoration services.

When looking for such a venue, find out where they source their food from. Ideally, the food should be locally-sourced, organic, and fair-trade compliant. Similarly, for decorations, options should prioritize reusable, recyclable, or biodegradable materials.

4.7. Planning Ahead

If you're planning a green wedding well in advance, you might consider supporting the development of a sustainable venue.

This could mean investing in the construction or renovation of a community garden, building, or park where you can host your wedding. Not only would this venue embody your commitment to the environment, but it would also leave a legacy and contribute beneficially to your local community.

In the end, remember that any healthy relationship, including the one with our planet, is rooted in compromise. It's about finding a balance between your dream wedding and the least harmful way of turning that dream into reality.

Understand that perfection might not be achievable, but each green choice you make is an affirmative nod to sustainability. You would be surprised to learn how these small choices can inspire big changes. Happy green venue hunting!

Chapter 5. Creating an Eco-friendly Wedding Checklist

Planning a wedding involves much detail, from venue selection to the menu, as all the elements mindfully come together to create your fairy tale day. Equally, the challenge of planning a sustainable wedding involves many intricate details, each carrying its own weight and impact on the environment. As such, we bring you a comprehensive checklist to ensure your wedding day is as green as can be.

5.1. Understand Your Carbon Footprint

The first step in planning a 'green' wedding is to understand the term 'Carbon Footprint.' It's a measure of the impact human activities have on the environment in terms of the amount of greenhouse gases produced, measured in tons of CO2. The smaller the footprint, the better. It means you're mitigating your contribution to global warming. Before beginning to plan your eco-friendly wedding, you should consider:

1. Engage with a carbon calculator: Websites, both free and premium, offer carbon calculators that can provide an estimate of emissions based on your daily activities.

2. Offsetting your carbon footprint: Offset your emissions by investing in sustainable initiatives. Several organizations have programs where you can purchase carbon offset credits.

5.2. Choose a Green Venue

If you pick a venue that is committed to sustainability, half of your work is done. Here are a few considerations:

1. Outdoor venues: Weddings under the open sky or in a garden can minimize the energy consumption of electrical lighting and air conditioning.

2. Multipurpose venues: A venue that can host both the ceremony and the reception will cut down on transportation.

3. Eco-certified venues: Look for venues with recognized environmental certifications.

4. Venues with an environmental cause: Some venues donate a part of their profits to environmental causes.

5.3. Opt for Ethical and Sustainable Wedding Attire

Your wedding attire contributes significantly to the carbon footprint of the event. You can reduce this by opting for ethical and sustainable options.

1. Look for vintage or second-hand dresses/suits: These options can save a garment from going to waste while keeping your carbon footprint low.

2. Choose a designer who uses environmentally friendly practices: These include using organic materials, natural dyes, or more energy-efficient manufacturing processes.

3. Rent your dress/suit: Several businesses offer rental services for bridal gowns and groom's suits.

4. Introduce the concept to your wedding party: Encourage them to choose eco-friendly options.

5.4. Design a Sustainable Menu

Your wedding menu is another vital aspect where you can significantly reduce your carbon footprint.

1. Opt for local and seasonal foods: It minimizes the carbon footprint linked to food transportation.

2. Caterers who prioritize sustainability: Look for caterers who incorporate sustainable practices into their services.

3. Vegan or Vegetarian options: Animal farming is one of the largest contributors to greenhouse gases. Therefore, offering vegan or vegetarian dishes at your wedding can help reduce carbon emissions.

4. A 'zero waste' meal: Request your caterer to create a menu that produces minimal waste.

5.5. Eco-friendly Invitations

Extend the boundaries of your sustainable thinking to your wedding invites.

1. E-invites: Save on paper by sending out digital invites.

2. Recycled Paper: For tradition's sake, if you still prefer physical invites, use recycled paper or cards embedded with seeds that can be planted.

3. Minimal design: Limit the number of pages and information on your physical invites to keep material usage to the bare minimum.

5.6. Sustainable Decor

The decor at your wedding venue sets the ambiance but can often become a source of considerable waste.

1. Hire: Opt for rented decor items instead of purchasing them.

2. Biodegradable materials: Use decor items made of biodegradable materials like jute, bamboo, etc.

3. Natural elements: Opt for decor made from organic materials such as locally sourced flowers, leaves, and stones.

5.7. Eco-friendly Wedding Favors

The tradition of giving wedding favors is delightful, but often these gifts end up contributing to waste.

1. Choose sustainable gifts: Opt for gifts made from sustainable or recycled materials.

2. Donate: Make a donation in the name of your guests to an environmental cause.

3. Plantable favors: You could consider giving out tree saplings or seeds, which can be planted by your guests.

5.8. Concluding Thoughts

In the end, while this checklist is comprehensive, it's merely a guide to get you started. There are countless additional ways you can reduce the carbon footprints of your wedding. It's all about being aware, thoughtful, and innovative with your planning while putting our planet first. Embrace the challenge and reap the rewards of hosting a truly sustainable wedding that leaves a lasting impression on your guests. You would inspire them not just with your love story but also with your commitment to the planet.

Ultimately, an eco-friendly wedding isn't just a one-day event. It's a commitment to sustainable living, a promise that goes beyond the 'I do's' and extends into the rest of your lives together.

Chapter 6. Sustainable Wedding Invitations and Stationery

Where the journey of every wedding starts is with both an announcement of love and the send-out of invites. Making these integral parts of a wedding sustainable is the fitting first step towards committing to an eco-friendly wedding.

6.1. Consider the Material

Our initial thought gravitates towards paper invitations and save-the-dates. However, before making that decision, it's important to always ponder over the impact it could have on the environment. Standard papers generally come from trees, contributing to deforestation. But fortunately, green alternatives are increasingly becoming available.

Recycled paper is a great option for eco-friendly wedding invitations. It uses less water and energy to produce than regular paper and diverts waste from landfills. Another option is plantable paper, a type of handmade paper that includes different plant seeds. When your guests plant these invitations in a pot of soil, the seeds germinate and sprout into small plants.

Other viable options are sustainably-sourced paper, tree-free paper made from crops such as bamboo or hemp, or cotton paper created from textile leftovers. Each option has its benefits and unique characteristics – sifting through them to find the perfect fit feels special in and of itself.

6.2. Minimize Waste with All-in-One Invitations

One invitation doesn't sound like a lot, but when you multiply it by every guest, the amount of paper and waste can add up. Consider choosing an all-in-one wedding invitation, which includes all your wedding information–the invitation, RSVP, reception details, accommodation information–in one neat package.

Guests tear off the RSVP postcard, keeping the rest as a single-page announcement. With fewer paper pieces, there's less waste, and the convenience of an all-in-one invite is appreciated by many guests.

6.3. Digital Invitations and e-RSVPs

A more radical way of reducing paper waste is by going digital. Websites and online platforms now offer a wide array of chic, customised digital invitation options that you can directly email to guests or share on social media. Electronic invitations are cost-saving, fast, and practical. The website can be your one-stop hub for all ceremony, reception details and updated news. It's a new-age solution that syncs well with a sustainable mindset.

Embracing technology doesn't end with invitations. Online RSVPs save paper and postage. Consider setting up a wedding website where guests can RSVP directly or utilize email for the same purpose.

6.4. Go Local

Choosing a local print shop to produce your invitations can reduce carbon emissions caused by shipping and support your local economy at the same time. Once you've decided on the type of eco-friendly paper and sign off on a design, finding a local craftsperson or printer to bring your creation to life can give your invites a personal touch. And who knows, their local knowledge might open doors to more sustainable solutions and vendors.

6.5. Choose Eco-Friendly Ink

Even the type of ink used to print your invitations can have an environmental impact. Traditional petroleum-based inks emit volatile organic compounds (VOCs) that contribute to pollution. Instead, look for inks made from food or soy-based materials. These inks are plant-derived and release fewer VOCs.

6.6. Keep it Simple

Simplicity can truly be the ultimate sophistication. Removing extra inserts, using a smaller card, or even shrinking the font size a bit can reduce the amount of paper used. Debossed or letterpress printing techniques can be used to maximize space further, allowing a larger font on smaller card sizes.

6.7. Post-Wedding Impact

Don't forget about potential waste once the wedding has passed. Encourage your guests to recycle invitations and other paper materials from the event. Consider adding a short line on your wedding stationery items about how to dispose of them responsibly. Something as simple as, "Please recycle this program after the ceremony" can prompt guests to think before simply discarding these items.

6.8. Personal Touches

Use the sustainability theme of your wedding as a decoration element for the invitations. Incorporate botanical themes or greenery illustrations, or even tie the bundle with a strip of vine or twine instead of a plastic ribbon. This way, the sustainability elements become an aesthetic choice and not just an environmental one.

6.9. Compact Forms

If you must use paper, look for compact form factors for invitations, such as a tri-fold invitation. This will ensure that all the essential details fit in, while reducing the paper footprint. Use clever design practices, such as print on both sides or use pockets, to make the most of the space available.

In summary, focusing on sustainability during each phase of your wedding's planning is an ideal way to honor and preserve our planet. Selecting eco-friendly wedding invitations and stationery is the perfect kickoff to your journey of green wedding planning. Ultimately, with these various considerations and actions, you'll create memorable invites that remind every guest the importance and urge of caring about our environment. Forever shall they remember your big day and the conscientious choices you curated it with.

Chapter 7. Organizing a Low Impact Wedding Reception: Food and Drinks

In every wedding reception, the food and drinks you serve play a major role. A sustainable wedding pushes us to think beyond the norm, to challenge the status quo, and consider innovative ways to cater to our guests, all while minimizing harm to our planet. This chapter will guide you through the complexities of organizing a food and beverages menu for a low-impact wedding reception.

7.1. Choosing Your Caterer Wisely

Partnering with a caterer who aligns with your vision of a green wedding is crucial. Search for caterers who prioritize local, seasonal, and organic produce. This not only reduces the meal's carbon footprint but also supports local farmers and promotes biodiversity.

Seek out caterers who are open to ideas like making your big day meatless, using only fair-trade ingredients, or cooking with minimal waste. Discuss with them about their waste management practices - do they recycle the waste produced from cooking, or better, do they compost it?

In larger cities, certain caterers specialize in sustainable practices and have previous experience with eco-friendly weddings. Prioritizing these businesses contributes to a greener economy and reduces your environmental impact.

7.2. Serve Seasonal and Local

The menu choices for your big day can make a significant difference.

Serving local and seasonal fare not only reduces the carbon footprint associated with long-distance transportation of food but also guarantees fresh and flavorful dishes.

Taking it a step further, consider having a meatless or vegan menu. Animal agriculture is one of the leading causes of carbon dioxide emissions, land degradation, and water pollution. Opting for a plant-based menu can significantly reduce your wedding's environmental impact.

7.3. Minimize Food Waste

According to the U.S. Environmental Protection Agency, food waste is one of the largest components of our trash, and weddings can be particularly wasteful events. However, careful planning can drastically reduce this waste.

It's helpful to confirm the number of guests few days before the wedding to avoid over-catering. If you still end up with leftovers, plan with your caterer how you'll manage them. Perhaps you can donate untouched food to a local food bank or compost leftovers.

Offering a choice of meals (meat, vegetarian, vegan) on the RSVP allows you plan exactly how much of each dish needs to be prepared, reducing the risk of excess.

7.4. Choose Organic Wine and Local Brews

Maintain your eco-friendly ethos when it comes to the bar as well. Opt for organic wines, which are made without synthetic pesticides and fertilizers. If beer is on the menu, consider local breweries. Not only does this reduce shipping emissions, but local businesses usually craft their drinks with high quality, often organic, ingredients.

7.5. Cut out Single-Use Items

When you're serving food and drinks, it's easy to produce a large amount of waste from single-use items. Opt for rented glassware, crockery and linen napkins over disposable plates, cups and napkins. If disposables are unavoidable, ensure they are made from renewable resources and are compostable.

7.6. Practicality and Purpose with Fair Trade

You can add more meaning to your sustainable reception by choosing fair trade products. They ensure fair wages to small-scale farmers and factory workers in developing countries. Coffee, chocolate, sugar, and some types of alcohol are commonly available in fair trade versions.

Choosing a green wedding doesn't mean you have to compromise on taste, quality, or aesthetics. With careful planning and thoughtful decisions, you can have a low-impact, environmentally friendly wedding reception that's still as magical and memorable as you'd always hoped it would be.

Chapter 8. Dressing for the Green Big Day: Eco-Conscious Apparel

The momentous wedding day deserves outfits that not only make you feel like royalty but also honor your commitment towards a sustainable future. This chapter delves into a range of avenues you can explore to acquire eco-conscious attire for your green big day.

8.1. Choosing Sustainable Materials

One significant aspect of picking out an eco-friendly dress or suit is emphasizing sustainable materials, such as organic cotton, bamboo, hemp, and silk, produced under fair-trade conditions.

Organic cotton is grown using methods and materials that have a low impact on the environment. This means it's free from toxic pesticides and fertilizers, and its cultivation process conserves water. Dresses made of organic cotton are typically very comfortable and breathable.

Bamboo fabric is renowned for its softness and durability. It has a naturally loose drape and a slightly shiny surface, making it an ideal material for chic wedding attire.

Hemp, though an uncommon fabric choice for some, offers superior durability and breathability. Hemp grows quickly, requires no chemicals to thrive, and is a fantastic choice for environmentally conscious clothing.

Silk, despite its opulent reputation, can be a sustainable choice. The peace silk (or Ahimsa silk) is processed from cocoons without killing the pupae inside, making it a cruelty-free silk option.

Look for the certified organic and fair-trade labels when shopping, as these certifications ensure that the materials were grown, harvested, and processed with both the environment and workers' wellbeing in mind.

8.2. Finding Eco-Friendly Designers

Countless eco-friendly designers are creating stunning wedding attire without cutting corners on sustainability. Designers like Leanne Marshall, Minna, and Sanyukta Shrestha are well-known in the industry for their ethical and environmentally considerate creations. Research for a designer whose ethos aligns with your values and whose designs speak to your aesthetic sensibilities.

8.3. Considering Pre-Loved Dresses

There is an undeniable charm and romance in giving a second life to a pre-loved wedding dress. Online platforms like Stillwhite and Nearly Newlywed offer gently worn designer wedding gowns at a fraction of their original price. Opting for a vintage or pre-loved dress not only makes eco-sense – extending the lifecycle of the garment – but can also help you acquire a unique piece with a story attached.

8.4. Discovering Dress Renting

Renting wedding attire is another remarkable way to reduce the environmental impact of your big day. Companies such as Rent the Runway and Borrowing Magnolia offer a diverse array of styles and designers for both brides and grooms. Renting reduces garment waste by encouraging the reuse of wedding attire and also affords you the luxury of donning a designer dress or suit without the hefty price tag.

8.5. Altering a Family Heirloom

Repurposing a family heirloom, such as your mother's or grandmother's wedding dress, is another sustainable, sentimental option. Discuss this idea with a local seamstress or tailor, who will be able to offer valuable suggestions on modernizing and customizing the dress to your liking.

8.6. Opting for Locally Made Dresses

Supporting a local designer or tailor not only boosts local economy and artisans but also reduces your carbon footprint by eliminating long-distance shipping. Look for bridal salons or designers in your local area, and make sure to ask about their production methods and supply chain.

8.7. Making Conscious Choices for Accessories

Your commitment to an eco-conscious wedding need not stop at the dress or suit. From your shoes to your jewelry, each element can align with your green values. Look for shoes made with sustainable materials or better, shop vintage. As for the jewelry, consider ethically sourced gems, recycled metals, heirloom pieces, or even lab-grown diamonds.

8.8. Ensuring Sustainable Practices for Your Bridal Party

Your bridal party can also follow suit (pun intended) in wearing sustainable attire. Encourage your party to select dresses or suits from eco-friendly designers, look into rental options, or pick attire that they would love to wear again.

Every effort counts when planning an eco-friendly wedding. Remember, the goal here is to reduce the negative footprint of your big day, not to achieve perfection. With your continued commitment to sustainability, your wedding day will be an unforgettable celebration of love, not just for each other, but also for the planet.

Chapter 9. Eco-Friendly Wedding Decor: Style Meets Sustainability

Weddings are a beautiful representation of love, commitment, and shared dreams. They're also an excellent opportunity to showcase personal style and, these days, a couple's shared values. Maybe you're an eco-conscious duo who craves to reduce the environmental footprint of your wedding day. Well, good news! That intention fits perfectly within the realm of wedding décor, where style can genuinely meet sustainability.

9.1. Sustainable Materials for Decor

Amongst the first steps you can take in planning eco-friendly wedding décor is to prioritize sustainable materials. Traditional décor often calls for a hefty amount of single-use items, many of which are plastic-based and contribute to waste.

To reduce your impact:

1. Opt for biodegradable materials like paper or bamboo over plastic.

2. Seek out decorations made from recycled materials.

3. Choose natural items, such as seasonal flowers and plants, fruits, vegetables, and natural fibers like cotton or linen.

4. Avoid non-recyclables such as Styrofoam or certain kinds of plastic.

5. Consider décor pieces that are made from reclaimed or upcycled items.

One popular trend is to use locally sourced flowers and greenery, combined with reusable items like glass jars, candles, and antique pieces that will still look delightful after the wedding day.

9.2. Secondhand but First Class

Thrift shops, garage sales, estate sales, and websites like Craigslist or Freecycle can be gold mines for perfect secondhand wedding décor. You can find everything you need - from tablecloths and candle holders to vases and old picture frames. Shopping secondhand for your items isn't just a way to save money; it's also a great way to make sure no new resources are wasted in creating your wedding decorations.

Also, don't underestimate the value of borrowing items from friends, family, or community members. This again reduces the need for new items and fosters a sense of community involvement in your big day.

9.3. Choose Renewable Over Disposable

There are many ways to avoid disposable wedding décor. Candles, for example, can be replaced with solar or battery-operated lights. You can also rent many items - like linens, tableware, even centerpieces – instead of buying them new.

If you choose disposables, look for eco-friendly alternatives. For example, you can use biodegradable confetti or rose petals instead of plastic confetti. Compostable tableware is becoming more affordable and readily available.

9.4. Minimalist Décor: Less is More

Embracing minimalism in your wedding décor is another way to reduce the environmental impact. Less clutter on tables means less manufacturing, less waste, and often less money spent. Use fewer items, but choose them carefully so each piece truly adds to your event's style and ambience.

A minimalist aesthetic includes utilizing the natural beauty of your venue. A beach doesn't need much decoration, nor does a garden or a forest. Capitalize on your natural surroundings to save on resources.

9.5. The Flowers: Wild, Local, and Seasonal

Flowers can have a significant environmental impact, considering the water, pesticides, and transport involved. Opt for organic, local, and in-season blooms to reduce your footprint. Consider using more greenery and fewer flowers, or use potted plants that can be reused or given to guests as gifts after the wedding.

9.6. The Power of DIY and Upcycling

Embrace your creativity by making your own wedding decorations from upcycled materials. Repurposed pallet wood can become directional signs, vintage teacups could hold tealights, and old books could be stacked to form unique table centerpieces. DIY also adds a personal touch to your day.

9.7. Décor with Longer Life: Give and Reuse

Choose décor that can be reused, repurposed, or donated after the wedding. For example, if you use fairy lights, they can decorate your home afterward. Table centerpieces or potted plants could become part of your guests' home décor.

9.8. Eco-Friendly Favors

For guests, consider eco-friendly options such as locally made soaps, homemade jams, or seed packets for native plants. Not technically décor, but displayed and presented creatively, they can double up as decoration and a parting gift.

9.9. Ethical Vendors

Many wedding suppliers understand that couples are more eco-conscious and are offering greener options. Find vendors who share your values. They should be able to provide you with eco-friendly options and give advice on the best choices for you.

9.10. Practical Note: Reusable Signage

Rather than using one-time-use signage or programs, go digital or choose reusable options. Consider chalkboards, mirrors, or other reusable items for your signage.

Hopefully, this comprehensive guide provides you with the inspiration and practical advice to realize your sustainable wedding decor dreams. Remember, every small step you take towards sustainability is a statement about your values and your shared commitment – as a couple – to preserve our beautiful planet for future generations.

Chapter 10. Sociably Sustainable: Gifts, Favors, and Registry Ideas

In the plight to keep our planet healthy, every aspect of our daily lives must be brought into question, even our weddings. Given that weddings involve many elements with high environmental impact potential, they can be a fertile place to implement our sustainable practices. From gifts to guest favors to registries, there are virtually limitless ways to make these aspects of your big day more sociably sustainable. By doing so, we not only create memorable events but also contribute to the larger purpose of environmental conservation.

10.1. Consciously Choosing Your Wedding Gifts

Wedding gifts are a tradition that dates back centuries. However, we must rethink how we participate in this tradition in an environmentally sound way. Fortunately, it's not difficult, and it doesn't necessitate forgoing gifts altogether.

Choose gifts that are made sustainably or buy from companies that employ sustainable practices. Brands are now paying more attention to their environmental footprint, and that extends to their products. Fairly traded goods, driftwood art, recycled jewellery, and even gifts made from vegan materials are now more accessible than ever. These gifts are unique indicating that a lot of thought and effort went into selecting them while remaining environmentally friendly.

You might also consider experiences rather than physical commodities. Think outside the box: what about a cooking course, a music festival ticket, or a year's subscription to a yoga studio?

10.2. Greener Gifting: Eco-Friendly Gift Wrapping

Let's not overlook the packaging. Traditional wrapping papers, especially if they are glittery or glossy, are often non-recyclable. Consider eco-friendly wrapping options such as reusable gift bags, cloth wraps (a method known as Furoshiki), or even newspaper. Refrain from using plastic ribbons and bows, and instead opt for compostable twines or simple paper raffia.

Moreover, including a note about the sustainable wrappers might encourage your guests to reuse or recycle them correctly.

10.3. Sustainable Wedding Registry Ideas

Wedding registries can be a prime target for sustainability. Registries inherently encourage consumption, so brides and grooms invested in sustainability should approach them wisely.

A sustainable wedding registry engages guests in your journey towards a more eco-conscious lifestyle. You can register for environmentally friendly goods or experiences. It also serves as a platform for encouraging others to consider how they consume and to perhaps reconsider their own lifestyle choices.

Consider adding the following types of products to your registry:

1. Eco-friendly appliances: Energy-star certified appliances, LED lighting fixtures, and other efficient tools.

2. Sustainable home goods: Organic cotton bed linens, reusable glass storage containers, and bamboo kitchen utensils.

3. Experiences: Rather than physical gifts, consider registering for

experiences such as cooking classes, nature retreats, or sports experiences.

4. Donations: As part of your registry, encourage guests to donate to environmental causes close to your heart.

10.4. Low-Waste Wedding Favors

Wedding favors are another area where we can express our commitment to sustainability. The concept of wedding favors is to give back. Why not give back to the planet as well?

Traditional wedding favors—small decorative items, often made of plastic—can be wasteful, ending up discarded after the event. Think, instead, of favors that are either useful, edible, or can be planted.

1. Edible treats: Miniature jars of honey from a local apiary, homemade biscotti in paper bags, or seeds for homegrown herbs in compostable containers.

2. Plantables: Small potted succulents, seed flyers, or tree saplings that can be planted.

3. Eco-usable items: Reusable tote bags, bamboo coffee cups, or beeswax food wraps.

Don't forget to let your guests know why you've chosen these sustainable options. This can be included in a little note with each favor or announced at the reception, creating more awareness and possibly setting a greener example for others to follow.

The journey to a green wedding starts with small, mindful steps. It is about creating an event dipped in meaning while cutting down on waste, and it encourages us, and our guests, to make more conscious choices. This journey might not be without its challenges, but the rewards of choosing an eco-friendly path far outweigh the hurdles. Sustainability is, after all, the ultimate celebration of love—for each other and for our world. Take part in this incredible movement, and let your wedding be the seed that sows change in your community.

Chapter 11. Saying Goodbye Sustainably: Honeymoon and Post-Wedding Best Practices

After the flurry of wedding activities, it's time to focus on the future—the honeymoon and what lies beyond. The decisions you make in your post-wedding life can have a significant impact on our planet. From where you choose to honeymoon to how you deal with unused wedding items, each choice can contribute to a healthier, more sustainable world.

11.1. Eco-friendly Honeymoon Destinations

Eco-tourism is gaining in popularity, with many facilities now offering sustainable travel options. These establishments often promote environmental conservation, support local economies, and champion indigenous cultures.

One breath-taking choice is Costa Rica's Pacuare Lodge. Nestled in sustainable luxury, this destination has won numerous awards - every aspect emphasizes sustainability, from the eco-adventures to the locally sourced meals.

For those more inclined towards a European vibe, the Whitepod Eco-Luxury Hotel in Switzerland provides an impressive model of sustainable hospitality. Its carbon-neutral pods deliver a carbon-efficient stay without compromising comfort and luxury.

Exploring the United States? Take a look at the sustainably designed huts of the Maine Huts & Trails system which offer guests an opportunity to experience remarkable landscapes while respecting natural resources.

11.2. Low-Impact Travel Options

Traveling to your honeymoon can also leave a carbon imprint. Consider the following practical ways to lessen your environmental footprint:

1. Carpooling or shared rides. It's not only an environment-friendly option but also a cost-effective one.

2. Public transport. This is another carbon-efficient alternative, especially in countries with well-planned travel systems.

3. Biking or walking. If your honeymoon venue is within reach, why not use the opportunity to get in a bit of exercise?

4. Carbon-offset flights. Some airlines provide options to make your air travel carbon-neutral through offset schemes. This involves investments in environmental projects to balance out your carbon emissions.

Remember to consider the most efficient travel route. Non-stop flights, for instance, are more fuel-efficient compared to flights with multiple stops.

11.3. Sustainable Lifestyles after the Wedding

Your commitment to sustainability shouldn't end after the wedding ceremony. Where appropriate, try to incorporate eco-friendly habits into your new life together.

1. Less is More: Minimalistic living means less waste and lower energy consumption. A minimalist lifestyle might involve sharing one vehicle, downsizing your living space, or purchasing fewer,

higher quality items that last longer.

2. Energy efficiency: Invest in energy-saving appliances and consider renewable energy sources such as solar panels.

3. Consume sustainably: Support brands with eco-friendly practices, and opt for ethical products. For instance, choose organic food or items made from recycled or sustainably-sourced materials.

11.4. Recycling Wedding Items

Try to repurpose, recycle, or donate leftover items from your wedding.

1. Donate: Charitable organizations often accept table decoration and wedding wear. Bridal gowns can have a second life in the hands of budget-conscious brides or for use in textile recycling.

2. Sell: Online platforms may be useful for selling wedding items that are in good condition. This not only recaptures some costs but also prevents the production of new items.

3. Repurpose: Transform your wedding items into keepsakes. Your bridal bouquet might be dried and framed, centerpieces can become home decor, and leftover candles can be used for romantic dinners at home.

11.5. Green Gifting

Even after the wedding, gifts will be part and parcel of your joint life—birthdays, anniversaries, and other significant occasions. Consider:

1. Eco-friendly gift options. These might be items that aid in reducing waste, like a stylish set of reusable shopping bags or bamboo toothbrushes.

2. Experience gifts. Instead of material items, opt for unforgettable

experiences, such as cooking classes, yoga retreats, or nature adventures.

11.6. Building Sustainable Traditions

Building a cultural legacy founded on sustainability, love, and respect for the environment can cement your lifelong commitment—not just towards each other, but also towards your global community. Choose locally grown food for your family feast days, participate in community clean-ups, and make eco-friendliness the norm in your household.

11.7. Embracing a Sustainable Mindset

Sustainability is more than a one-off event or a check-marked box in the "good deeds" bracket. It's a shift in thinking that permeates every aspect of daily life. The sustainable couple considers ethics and environmental impact in all their choices—from what's in their wardrobe and cupboards to where their investment money goes.

Overall, planning a sustainable honeymoon and post-wedding life relies on thoughtful decisions and actions. Seize this opportunity to make a lasting difference, celebrate your love, and honor the precious planet we all share. Let your wedding be the starting point of a beautiful journey towards sustainability that inspires other couples in their journey. You've said 'I do' to each other; now it's time to say 'I do' to the earth.